WOW!
Forests

A Book of Extraordinary Facts

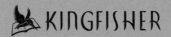

KINGFISHER

First published 2020 by Kingfisher
an imprint of Macmillan Children's Books
The Smithson, 6 Briset Street, London EC1M 5NR
Associated companies throughout the world
www.panmacmillan.com

Author: Camilla de la Bédoyère
Design and styling: Liz Adcock
Jacket design: Liz Adcock
Natural history consultant: Camilla de la Bédoyère
Illustrations: Ste Johnson

ISBN 978-0-7534-4542-6

Copyright © Macmillan Publishers International Ltd 2020

1 3 5 7 9 8 6 4 2
1TR/0320/WKT/UG/140WFO

A CIP catalogue record for this book is available from the British Library.

Printed in China

WOW! Forests

A Book of Extraordinary Facts

KINGFISHER

Terrific trees!

Take a stroll through the forest and find out just how fabulous it is...

There are up to three trillion (3,000,000,000,000) trees here on planet Earth. Most of them are in forests and woodlands. They cover one-third of Earth's land and are home to all sorts of wildlife.

Forests around the world

Tropical Rain Forest

Temperate Forest

Evergreen Forest

A tree is a woody plant that grows tall. It has roots, a trunk that is covered in tough bark and branches that bear lots of leaves.

4

Wow!

The leaves on a raphia palm tree can grow up to 25 metres long. That's three times longer than a bus!

Wow!

Even the mightiest tree begins life as a seed, and most seeds are no bigger than your thumb.

Up, up, UP!

The biggest trees are giant sequoias. It would take about 20 children holding hands to circle the huge trunks of the oldest trees. Their bark can grow 30 centimetres thick.

Trees don't eat. Like other plants, they make their own food. They use sunlight, water and carbon dioxide in the air to do this. It's called photosynthesis, which means 'making with light'.

what's this?

5

Wonderful woodlands

Woodlands need soil, seeds, plenty of rain and warm sun. They are home to lots of tree-loving animals!

Woodlands grow in places where there are seasons and the weather is never too hot, too dry or too cold.

I'm **Pando**, the trembling giant!

Wow!

In the autumn, aspen leaves turn yellow. When the wind passes through their leaves they tremble, quake and shake, making a sound like rustling whispers...

Pando is a forest of aspen trees that are all connected by their roots, making one enormous living thing! It's believed to be 80,000 years old.

I've been very busy this year!

An oak tree can grow half a million leaves and 10,000 acorns in just one year. That's hard work!

Tap, tap, tap.

Acorn woodpeckers collect acorns and store them in holes in oak trees so they have food in the winter. One tree was found with 50,000 acorns in it!

Koalas spend all day munching on the leaves of a eucalyptus tree. When they're not eating, they can spend up to 18 hours a day sleeping!

Eat, sleep, repeat...

Bats and bugs

From the tips of the leaves to the tops of the trees, there are busy bats and bugs to see.

This is a baobab tree. It has a big trunk and thick branches that look more like roots. Its white flowers turn brown and start to stink. It's a smell that bats love!

I'm called the upside-down tree.

At mating time, male stag beetles use their huge jaws to battle each other. They can't use these jaws to eat, so they don't live more than a few weeks!

Fight, fight!

Giant golden orb-web spiders spin their webs between trees. They can be more than 150 centimetres wide! These webs are strong enough to catch big bugs, bats and even small birds!

Mmm... bats are tasty!

Peepo!

Some bats use tree leaves to build themselves a tent! Their leafy home keeps them dry when it rains.

whoosh!

Hundreds of eastern tent caterpillars work together to coat an entire tree with silk. This silken tent protects them from birds while they devour the tree's leaves.

we are the munch bunch!

Wow!

The largest bats are flying foxes, or fruit bats. They measure 170 centimetres from wing-tip to wing-tip!

Mangrove forests

These forests grow where the land meets the sea, and trees dip their roots in salty water.

Wow!

The largest salties are 3 metres long and have 66 big pointy teeth.

Mangrove trees have long roots that look like stilts. They suck up seawater and squeeze the salt out of their leaves and branches!

I see you, tiger!

Saltwater crocodiles – or 'salties' – live in mangrove forests. They hide in water and wait for fish to swim past, but they have been known to hunt even bigger prey, including humans and tigers!

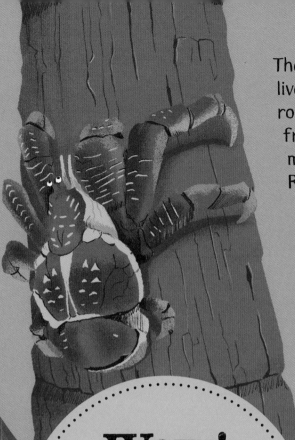

The heaviest crabs in the world live in mangrove forests. These robber crabs measure a metre from toe to toe and weigh as much as four bags of sugar! Robber crabs climb trees to reach coconuts.

Watch out below!

Wow!

The Sundarbans Mangrove Forest is home to 177 types of fish, 24 types of shrimp and more than 300 different types of plant.

The world's largest seeds come from a palm tree that grows along mangrove coasts. The tree is called the coco-de-mer and each nut weighs as much as a 10-year-old child.

Whose tail is this?

Better keep away from that salty!

Tigers love to wallow in the swampy water. They can climb, run and swim, so watch out!

Meet the monkeys

Monkeys love trees! They hang out in forests and swing through the branches.

Langur monkeys have big bellies and burp a lot! Their babies are bright orange and change colour as they get older.

Hic! Pardon me!

Did you know?

Monkeys and apes belong to a group of animals called primates. They have hands for gripping and their eyes face forwards, just like us!

My nose is so big that when I jump it flies up and hits me in the face!

Proboscis monkeys live in trees by rivers, where they like to take a cooling swim on hot days. Babies are born with blue faces and the male monkeys have huge noses!

I love to swing about!

Gibbons swing through the forest at 50 kilometres an hour. They almost fly through the air between trees, covering a distance of 15 metres in a single swing!

Just hanging around.

Some monkeys have long tails that they can wrap around branches. This lets them hang upside down!

Thanks for the piggyback ride, dad.

Tamarins are mini-monkeys that often have moustaches – even the mums! They give birth to twins and dad gives them a piggyback.

Evergreen forests

There are ancient giants living in evergreen forests — the oldest and tallest trees alive.

Evergreen forests in cool parts of the world are full of conifer trees that don't lose their leaves in winter. They can cope with snow, cold and wind, and long dry spells when there's little rain.

we're just fine in the snow.

Evergreen forests are home to animals with some cunning defences...

i'm dead, honestly!

Spotted skunks do handstands to spray a foul liquid at an attacker with perfect aim!

Keep back!

Virginia opossums pretend they are dead when they are attacked. They roll over and stick out their tongues!

14

The world's largest tree is bigger than the Statue of Liberty, in New York, USA. It's a coast redwood in California and is about 116 metres tall. Called Hyperion, this giant might have grown taller, but woodpeckers damaged its top!

Taller than me!

Wow!
Trees can live to a great age. Some bristlecone pines are at least 4800 years old!

Wow!
There are huge forests of conifer trees in North America and Russia. They are called taiga, or boreal forests. The Russian taiga is so big that it takes a week to travel past it by train!

Bears everywhere!

There are eight types of bear and all of them except polar bears can be found in forests and woodlands.

DO I look a bit spooky?

Ghostly white bears live in the Great Bear Rainforest of Canada. They are called Kermode bears, or spirit bears.

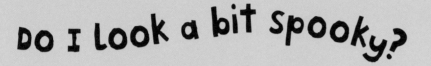

I love bamboo!

Panda bears live in bamboo forests. They eat more than 60 different types of bamboo, but that's almost all they eat! One panda munches through 2,000 bamboo stems a day.

Wow!

A panda poos a hundred times a day!

Most bears love climbing trees, especially when they are cubs. Spectacled bears sleep in trees, sloth bears like to hang upside down from a branch and sun bears make nests from branches and leaves.

ZZZZZZZ....

Hi down there!

SLurrrrpppp!

Many bears spend the winter asleep in a den. This is called hibernation. American black bears like to hibernate in tree holes.

Sloth bears are noisy eaters. They can be heard 180 metres away, slurping and sucking up termites from a rotten log!

Watch out for the bear!

17

Rainforests

Rainforests are the some of the world's most precious places. They buzz with life! The plants in a rainforest grow in three levels.

Rainforests grow in warm places where there is rain most days. They are steamy, hot and full of lush green plants reaching up to the sky. Some trees grow taller than a ten-storey building!

Harpy eagles are so big they can hunt monkeys and sloths!

The tallest trees poke above the canopy, reaching the sunlight. This is called the **emergent layer.**

The **canopy layer** is a massive blanket of green, made up of the branches and leaves of older trees.

Emergent layer

Sloths hang upside down from rainforest trees. They move so slowly that tiny plants grow in their fur, turning them green. Once a week they crawl to the ground to poo!

wow!
About two-thirds of rainforest animals and plants live in the canopy!

Canopy layer

Jaguars are large jungle cats that hunt sloths and wild pigs. Their jaws are so strong they can crush bone.

It's hot, steamy and dark near the forest floor. This is the **understorey**, where shrubs and young trees fight for light.

Understorey

Forest frogs

It's easy to hear a frog in a forest, but hard to find one. Beware of the colourful ones!

Frogs are amphibians, which means they live both on land and in water. They have soft, moist skin and prefer wet places. Forests can be good places for frogs to stay damp and out of sight.

Wow!
Glass frogs are see-through! Some of them have red tadpoles that live in mud and wet leaves under trees, instead of in a pond or river.

Ribbit! Ribbit!

At breeding time, male frogs and toads croak loudly to tell their mates where to find them. They use air to make their throat pouches swell up like balloons, which helps their voices to travel far.

Most frogs lay their eggs in water.
Tadpoles are baby frogs that hatch from
the eggs. They have tails for swimming
and look very different to their parents!

I have suckers on my feet!

we'll be frogs one day!

Red-eyed tree frogs have sucker-like pads
on their feet. They climb upside down and lay
their eggs on the underside of leaves. When
the eggs hatch, the tadpoles drop into the
river below. The baby frogs grow legs
and clamber back into the tree.

My skin is pretty, but deadly!

Most tree frogs are green so they
can hide, but poison arrow frogs
prefer to be noticed. Their bright
colours tell predators that their
skin is coated in deadly poison.
If you lick one of these frogs
you could die very quickly...
so don't ever lick a frog!

Peculiar plants

Take a peek at some amazing plants that grow in the cool shade of woodlands and forests.

My belly hurts!

Macaws love nibbling on the poisonous seeds of a hura tree. As soon as they've finished their meal they fly to a riverbank, where they eat special clay that cures their stomach-ache!

So yummy, but SO smelly!

Durian fruits smell like dead fish and stinky poo. Orangutans love them!

When a bug lands on a Venus flytrap, its leaves snap shut, trapping the bug inside. The plant turns the bug into mush and eats it.

HELP!

Forest flowers can be enormous. Titan arums grow flower stalks that are 3 metres tall and the rafflesia flower is a metre wide! It smells like rotting meat, which is the favourite smell of the flies that pollinate it.

POO!

Buzz! Buzz!

Bee orchid flowers look and smell just like female bees! It's a clever trick to make sure they get pollinated. Male bees land on the flowers hoping to mate with them, but get covered with pollen instead.

Wow!

When plants 'hear' caterpillars munching on another plant nearby, they make nasty-tasting chemicals in their leaves to stop the caterpillars eating them too.

Best friends

Did you know that, over its lifetime, a single tree is a home and food for millions of animals?

Wow!

The Brazil nut tree is the largest tree in the Amazon rainforest. It grows 50 metres tall and can reach 1000 years old.

1 The Brazil nut tree grows white flowers from October to December. It can only be pollinated by certain types of bees, such as orchid bees that have long tongues to reach nectar deep inside the flower.

Buzz! Yummy!

2 After it's been pollinated, the flower begins to grow a fruit, but it's so big that this can take more than a year!

3 The Brazil nut fruit is a huge, hard pod that is as big and round as a cannonball. It's called a cocos and has a hard, woody shell. Inside are up to 25 Brazil nuts, each in another hard shell.

Found it!

4 When they're ripe and ready, the cocos fall to the forest floor where large rodents called agoutis collect them. Only an agouti has strong enough teeth to bite into a cocos and reach the nuts inside.

crunch!

5 Agoutis eat some nuts and bury others, saving them for later. If they forget where they buried their nuts, the nuts – which are seeds – grow into new Brazil nut trees.

The Brazil nut tree, the bees and the agoutis are best friends because they need each other to survive.

Sleepers and creepers

Shhh — it's night-time in the forest. See who's sleeping...and who's creeping through the trees.

Thousands of twinkling fireflies gather on rainforest trees near rivers. They light up the forest like fairy lights! These bugs are actually beetles, not flies, and they use lights to attract their mates.

My bum is so **shiny!**

Quick mum, lick my fur!

When a slow loris leaves her baby to go hunting for food she licks it first! She covers its fur with spit and a poison she makes in her skin. Now her baby tastes horrible to any predator.

I'll give the loris a miss tonight.

Clouded leopards love climbing trees. They use their long tail to balance and their long claws to grip tightly to branches as they leap through the forest.

Wolverines prowl through the forest at night. They're known as stink bears because they stink! They can climb trees, but they are related to skunks, not bears. These hunters will eat almost anything, including rotting meat and bones.

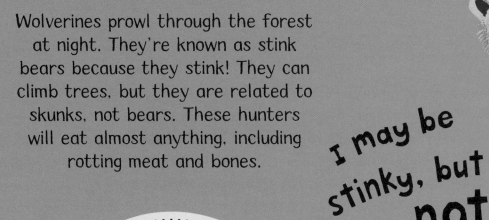

I may be stinky, but I am **not** a bear!

Did you know?

Rabbits burrow beneath tree roots and sleep there when owls and wolverines are out and about!

Most songbirds sleep at night, perching on branches. Woodpeckers use their strong beaks to make tree holes, where they rest and keep their chicks safe.

ZZZZZZ...

where do these go?

The forest floor

Look beneath your feet — there is a whole world of wildlife waiting to be discovered.

Many trees lose their leaves in autumn, when the weather turns cooler. The leaves lose their green colour and turn many shades of yellow, red and brown before falling to the ground.

Did you know?

Mini-beasts such as woodlice, ants, millipedes and slugs nibble away at rotting leaves and fallen branches.

A thick blanket of leaves under trees is called leaf litter and is home to many animals. When leaf litter rots, it turns into new soil where plants can grow.

I love stamping!

Tenrecs stamp on the ground to encourage earthworms to pop their heads up out of the leaf litter. When they're scared, tenrecs raise their spines and squeal loudly!

Wow!

Forest trees are connected to each other by fungi that grow around their roots. They use these fungi like a 'Wood Wide Web', sending messages to warn each other when tree-eating insects are about.

Mushrooms and toadstools belong to a group of living things called fungi. They grow inside rotting wood. turning it into food that they then suck up!

A group of 8 million ants can move 40 tonnes of soil while they build their underground nest.

We are very strong when we work together.

Forests are fab!

Forests are wonderful places where lots of animals and plants live — but humans need them too.

Forests help control the weather and keep the planet cool. Trees mop up carbon dioxide, which is the gas that is harming the atmosphere and making the world too warm. Their roots, leaves and bark help to remove pollution.

Ah, fresh air!

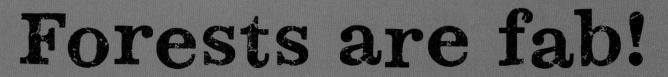

Did you know?

Every year, the world celebrates forests with a special day on 21 March — let's party!

More types of animal live in forests than anywhere else on land. Just one oak tree is home to more than 280 different types of insect.

About 1.5 million people live in rainforests. They get everything they need from their leafy home and many of them have never travelled outside of the forest.

Hello!

Mmm, coffee!

We use wood from trees to build houses and make paper, cardboard and furniture. Just one tree can be turned into 170,000 pencils or 8000 sheets of paper.

Mmm, chocolate!

Chocolate, coffee and rubber all come from trees, as well as all sorts of delicious fruits, berries and nuts.

Trees and me

Hug a tree and be happy!

All over the world, trees and forests are being cut down. Show trees how much you love them by giving one a hug! Just being around trees can make us feel peaceful and happy.

There are fewer than 400 Sumatran tigers left in the wild because their rainforest home has been cut down to grow oil palm trees instead.

I'm fighting for survival.

About 1.5 billion trees are chopped down each year. You can reduce this number by recycling paper. When you recycle paper, it gets turned into a soupy pulp that is made into new paper. Hooray!

I make a great home for bugs!

Make a bug home by creating a stack of old wood, twigs and piles of rotting leaves. The happy bugs that live there will pollinate living trees, which will then grow more seeds.